T0132255

A cancer survivor's stories of how
she saw God during her journey

PAULA GOWER

WestBow Press books may be ordered through booksellers or by contacting:

WestBow Press
A Division of Thomas Nelson & Zondervan
1663 Liberty Drive
Bloomington, IN 47403
www.westbowpress.com
844-714-3454

Interior Image Credit: Bianca Ambrosio

Scriptures are taken from the Holy Bible, New International Version®. NIV®. Copyright © 1973, 1978, 1984 by International Bible Society. Used by permission of Zondervan. All rights reserved.

ISBN: 978-1-6642-9874-3 (sc)
ISBN: 978-1-6642-9875-0 (hc)
ISBN: 978-1-6642-9876-7 (e)

Library of Congress Control Number: 2023907961

Print information available on the last page.

WestBow Press rev. date: 05/09/2023

WESTBOW
PRESS®
A DIVISION OF THOMAS NELSON
& ZONDERVAN

CONTENTS

I Saw God in a Phone Call

It had been five years since my last mammogram. Why? I cannot explain. You don't ever think you will be the one with cancer. It will be someone else, but not you. A dear friend of mine possibly saved my life by making me pick up the phone and make that first phone call to my doctor. When my friend Janet Smith heard that it had been five years since my last mammogram, she encouraged me to make an appointment. Sometimes you feel like that call can wait until tomorrow; then tomorrow comes, and it gets pushed back to the next day. We've all done it, in some manner. Maybe it's even as simple as mowing the lawn or unloading the dishwasher or filing your taxes, but we all put off things that we don't enjoy. It took five varying days of Janet coming into my classroom to ask me if I'd made my appointment before I finally did. She took my phone and pulled up the number so I wouldn't have any excuses.

With that phone call and mammogram, we found out that there was something there. What I didn't know was that God had a different path for me. My loving, caring Father was aware of my diagnosis long before I was aware of it. In His sovereignty, He placed specific people, each with a unique and meaningful purpose, into my path at varying points of my journey to take my hand and guide me through the difficult steps I had to take. He gave people different jobs, but each job was meaningful in its own way. God's hand was evident from the initial phone call all the way to the very end of this journey. I have learned that God is with me when I receive exciting and good news and when I receive news that will shake me to the core. Whatever the outcome would be, I trusted in His hand.

> For this God is our God for ever and ever; he will be
> our guide even to the end. (Psalm 48:14)

> The Lord will fulfill his purpose for me; your love,
> O Lord, endures forever. (Psalm 138:8)

CHAPTER 2
I Saw God in My Diagnosis

April 22, 2014 had to have been the hardest day I have lived through yet. I knew this would be the day I would receive my diagnosis. I couldn't even go to work out of fear of what I was going to hear on the other end of that phone call I knew I would receive. My sweet mother-in-law lovingly invited me over to her house so I wouldn't be alone. She tried her best to divert my thoughts and attention to something other than my worries. God also put Bonnie Eckles and Marcie Carter with me for the day. He knew just what I needed.

Then came the dreaded phone call and I heard the words, "Mrs. Gower, do you have someone with you right now?" I knew before she even finished her sentence what my diagnosis was. I don't even remember the rest of the telephone call, as the fear of this horrible disease ran through my every thought.

"Paula, you have cancer."

My heart sank into my stomach. How would I tell my kids? How would I tell my mom and brothers? My mother-in-law, Connie, and my friends Bonnie and Marcie were with me and held the hands of me and my husband while we made those difficult phone calls and told Daniel, my youngest, face-to-face. I had not expressed any previous concern to my children, so the news came as a huge surprise. Even though it came to us all by surprise, it did not take God by surprise. My story was written long ago. At the time, I did not know that He would equip me with everything I needed to fight this battle. He had been preparing me for a long time, giving me the spiritual, mental, and emotional strength each day to fight this thing to the end. He gave me the ability to hold my head up high during my journey.

Philippians 4:13 says, "I can do everything through him who gives me strength." Here, Paul says that he knows what it is like to have plenty and what it is like to have little; he knows what it means to be made high and then to be knocked down low. However, he believes that the one who grants his weary, mortal body with strength will carry him through whatever comes. The same applies to us. We need to find our strength in Jesus. He is our steady rock while everything else is blown and tossed by the wind.

CHAPTER 3
I Saw God in My Husband

Minutes after my diagnosis and the dreaded phone calls to family, my precious husband took charge of the situation and started making plans for what we were going to do next. He knew there was no way I could navigate the situation, and I love that he loved me so much that he didn't skip a beat. He was on the phone almost immediately and had me admitted to MD Anderson. He did every bit of the legwork, calling my local doctors to obtain whatever current files and scans they had. He arranged for hotels. He arranged for my twelve-year-old son to have loved ones to stay with while we were gone. Alan was not just there for me on the day of my diagnosis. He was there for my entire two-year journey. He taught Daniel how to do laundry. He did every bit of the grocery shopping. He would prepare my bed when he knew I did not have the physical strength to get in by myself. He rubbed peppermint oil on my stomach when I was nauseated. He had the knowledge to tell me to lie down and rest when he knew I was tired. He was my rock. He stepped in when he knew I could not stand alone.

My journal entry six days after my diagnosis said, "Found out today that my appointment is for next Thursday, May 8. I am so ready for the next step. I am so grateful for the man God gave me as my husband. He has been a trooper through this battle—and the fight is yet to come. I could not have asked for a more caring, loving, and compassionate husband. And who would have thought he could be so organized?" Without the strength of my God and my husband, I don't know what I would have done. Thank you, God, for knowing thirty-four years ago that I would need Alan to walk beside me through this journey.

He gives strength to the weary and increases the
power of the weak. (Isaiah 40:29)

CHAPTER 4
I Saw God in the Color Pink

After my breast cancer diagnosis, I had to figure out how I was going to navigate all of it. Phone calls and texts to loved ones were made with great difficulty, and within minutes of my diagnosis, my sweet husband and my mother-in-law were on the phone to MD Anderson trying to schedule my initial appointment. I'm telling you, word travels fast. It wasn't long before I started receiving phone calls, texts, and more support than one could imagine.

Two very dear friends, Donna McGraw and Wendy Humphries, came immediately to my rescue! They came over to my mother-in-law's house carrying a little care package lovingly compiled. Everything in the package was pink. They went the extra mile to make sure I knew they would be willing to walk with me through this journey. I am forever grateful for those two friends who also took the time to fly to Houston the following February to stay with me for a few days during my time there for radiation. They gave me the confidence I needed to go out in public for the first time without some sort of head covering following chemotherapy. With those two by my side, I knew I could conquer just about anything.

God taught me valuable things on the day of my diagnosis. Even though I felt discouraged and overcome with worry, as if my prayers were unanswered, I had to realize that there was no limit to what He could accomplish. I learned in the first three to four hours of diagnosis that I was not going to walk this road alone. I knew I had to change my mindset from the overwhelmingly negative to the unexplainable, positive hope that God was already showing me in just a short amount of time. I feel that the more extreme your circumstances, the more likely you are to see God show up at every corner. A friend taught me that the most outlandish works of God are seen in the most difficult of circumstances. God showed up during my journey, and that will be evident in each of the following chapters.

In Exodus chapters 3 and 4, we can read about a conversation between Moses and God. God informs Moses of the misery of his people in Egypt and His desire to rescue them from the hands of the Egyptians. He informed Moses of His intention to send him to Pharaoh to bring His people, the Israelites, out of Egypt. At least five times, Moses told God he was not equipped for this mission. He begged God to send someone else. God's response was, "I will be with you." Here, Moses did not feel equipped to do the work of his God because he was trying to figure out how to accomplish the task on his own. God kept reminding Moses that He would be with him. See, we *cannot* fight our battles alone. God will be with you through your journey. You must trust in His plan, not your own.

My goal in this short book is to show you how God was there for me through the whole journey. He met every need—needs I didn't even know I had. He held my hand when I needed it held. He wrapped His loving arms around me when I felt alone. He gave me friends and family to walk this journey with. I learned the importance of keeping my eyes and mind wide open so I could see what He was doing with every step.

Psalm 18:6 says, "In my distress I called to the Lord; I cried to my God for help. From his temple he heard my voice; my cry came before Him, into his ears."

Psalm 18:16 says, "He reached down from on high and took hold of me; he drew me out of deep waters."

CHAPTER 5
I Saw God in One Bite at a Time

The day after my diagnosis, Janet Smith, the same friend who made me make the phone call for my mammogram, came into my classroom at school. We teach together at the same school, and she is a longtime friend from college. I did not know that the words she would soon speak to me would forever change my life.

She asked me, "How do you eat an elephant?"

At the time, I had no clue what the answer was. She proceeded to tell me that you eat an elephant "one bite at a time." She told me not to worry about the whole journey because it would be too overwhelming. Just focus on one bite. Then, you can focus on your next bite, and before you realize it, your whole journey will be complete. Janet proceeded to tell me that Psalm 119:105 promises that "your word is a lamp unto my feet and a light for my path." This means that He is helping us with each step, one step at a time.

If you are wondering how you will get through today and how you will cope with all that is before you, you must go through this day like any other day: one step at a time. Keep your mind on your Father and take the next step. The more demanding your day is, the more He will guide you and walk with you. You will need to follow His lead and trust in Him.

Sometimes, I know that it is a challenge to make the most of every tick of the clock. I think serious news and details that make life take an immediate turn awaken us. In the midst of your storm, focus on renewing your hope in our never-failing, never-changing Father. When you do, you will find that your strength will be refreshed, and your purpose will be redefined. You will soar high instead of sinking deep. Hang in there and remember that God honors those who are faithful to His calling.

But those who hope in the LORD will renew their strength. They will soar on wings like eagles; they will run and not grow weary; they will walk and not be faint. (Isaiah 40:31)

CHAPTER 6
I Saw God in an Elephant

Not even thirty minutes after Janet left my classroom with her story on how to eat an elephant, a dear, sweet friend, Susan Rock, came into my classroom. Susan has to be the most giving, thoughtful person one could meet. She loves to give little gifts. None of them are of great value cost wise, but they are all of great value to my heart. Susan puts thought into each and every gift and knows just what you need and when you need it. Just about every day, Susan would come into my room, often bearing a small gift and always giving a hug and an "I love you!" This day in particular, Susan's gift meant more to me than any other gift I have or will ever receive.

I opened my little gift from Susan, and it just so happened to be a little elephant. I knew very quickly that there are no "just sos" with God. Everything He does, every scenario He orchestrates, is for a reason. I knew then that only God could have orchestrated this whole scenario, from Janet asking how to eat an elephant to Susan giving a gift of an elephant moments later. This was His way of letting me know that everything would be all right.

My new little elephant friend went with me to every chemo, every surgery, and every radiation treatment. He sat beside my table when I was at home. He was a good support for me during my two-year journey. Who would have known that a little elephant could change my life and the lives of so many more?

For those of you who do not know my story, about a year after my journey began, I decided to share my testimony with a friend. I decided to give her an elephant as well. Now, many years later, I have given hundreds of elephants to those receiving their dreadful diagnoses. This small ministry has now turned into a non-profit called One Bite at a Time Ministries. I try my best to help guide others in fighting cancer with faith over fear.

God is concerned with every detail of your life; He is always aware of you. He knows even the number of hairs on your head. He knows your whole story, even the parts that have not yet been written. We need to make sure that our focus is broad enough to include our Father in each and every thought. In return, we will feel safe and complete. Even though our lives are unstable, and our health is unstable, His love for us will never fail.

> "Are not two sparrows sold for a penny? Yet not one of them
> will fall to the ground apart from the will of your Father. And even
> the very hairs of your head are all numbered. So don't be afraid; you
> are worth more than many sparrows." (Matthew 10:29–31)

CHAPTER 7
I Saw God in My Friends

The abundant amount of texts, phone calls, gift baskets, prayers, and friends taking me to get coffee or tea blessed me greatly and carried me through the next few days. The waiting time between my diagnosis and my final appointment to finalize my treatment plan were brutal. Not knowing the severity of my cancer, not knowing if the cancer had spread, not knowing if I would live to see a grandchild or be present to watch my youngest son graduate from high school was more than I could take alone. I prayed that God would physically carry me through the few weeks and months that followed my diagnosis. Even now, when I am afraid or down, He sends someone with the exact words that I need. I am constantly reminded of the words from a favorite song, "Oh God you are my God, and I will ever praise you."

In the evenings, I would spend time alone with God journaling. The day after my diagnosis, in my journal I wrote, "I am overwhelmed by the people reaching out. From the phone calls, texts, gifts, cards, hugs, and tears shared, I am loved by so many people. God has blessed me beyond what I could have ever imagined."

There were days that I felt a gray cloud all around me. There were days I felt alone. There were days I was afraid, and there were days I didn't feel I had the strength to make it to the next day. However, on the days I felt like that, I asked God for reminders of His love. His love was shown in the people who did not know what to do or what to say, but they happened to have the perfect gift or words at the perfect time. God knew when I needed to be uplifted, and He used those specific people to get the job done. I want to challenge each one of you to watch for God's tender "I love you" in unexpected places and unexpected people. When you do see those unexpected circumstances, pause and give Him thanks.

You will seek me and find me when you seek me with all your heart. (Jeremiah 29:13)

CHAPTER 8
I Saw God in an Innocent Heart

One of my prayers during my journey was for me and my loved ones to see how God was working through all the shock and unknowns surrounding my diagnosis. The day before I left for my appointments at MD Anderson, I was flooded, once again, with much needed support. I had enough snacks and pajamas to last a month, thanks to all my sweet friends!

I prayed that my children would be able to see God throughout this whole season. I knew my youngest, Daniel, would have to bear the brunt of my days to come, as my oldest two were in Arkansas at school. I asked God to protect his sweet, tender heart and that God would be evident in our lives. I trusted that God would work in my children's lives as we walked this path.

Well, that prayer was answered very quickly. When Daniel saw all the love that was poured out on his mother during this time, he looked up at me with his sweet innocent heart and said, "Mom! It's all been worth it! Hasn't it?" I'm sure he was thinking about all the snacks and gifts. What twelve-year-old boy wouldn't? My first reaction was, well no! Having all the snacks in the world wouldn't fix cancer. I'm not going to lie; it was a good excuse to eat junk food! However, after I thought about it, that one statement alone did make cancer worth it. I knew that my child saw God in the lives of all my friends. He saw what having a community meant to someone in need. He finally realized that the support from your community was important and being a part of a Christian community is irreplaceable. I love how I saw God work in the life of my child that day. If you are not part of a community, I challenge you to become involved. Surviving hardships is much easier with community. God gave them to us for a reason.

Daniel blessed me not only that day, but throughout my treatments. In the evenings. I would go to bed to rest and reflect on the day. As I would listen to music and journal, I would look for ways that God blessed me each day, and seeking Scripture played a huge part in lifting me up. On some occasions, Daniel would come and get in bed to be with me. Sometimes we would talk, other times he would lay his head on my shoulder to let me know he was there for me. Sometimes, he would look for Scripture that he hoped would bless his mom. One of my favorite Scriptures he found was Proverbs 19:21: "Many are the plans in a man's heart, but it is the Lord's purpose that prevails". Thank you, Daniel, for the sweet times we had in the evenings and for caring enough to just sit and dwell on how the Lord is working in our lives.

CHAPTER 9

I Saw God in a Student

God gave me the gift of students to minister to me. Several students wrote sweet notes that I took to MD Anderson with me for my initial visit. I kept them in an envelope and saved them to open for much needed encouragement right before an appointment. I had so many that I still had some left over when I got home. What a blessing! One of the notes from a precious student really stuck out to me. In that letter, she wrote that upon hearing of my diagnosis, she wanted to remind me that I was chosen. This sweet student also wrote a specific prayer for me and my family. In that prayer, she affirmed that God knows every problem we have, and she asked God to watch over Alan, Hailey, Marcus, and Daniel. She asked that God reveal that I was strong. She said that I would be able to get through this road because she knew that God would be by my side. She wanted me to know through this prayer that no matter what the road ahead was, God would be with me no matter what. She affirmed that God already knew the plan for me and encouraged me to trust in Him. She ended with a reminder that I was chosen to walk this road with God. She knew that God had chosen His strongest soldier.

I did not know at the time, but the phrase "you were chosen" ended up being the theme for my journey. The fact that God chose me on April 22, 2014 to walk with Him gives me such comfort. He picked me up out of my normal, everyday life, and we walked together, hand in hand through the next two years. I would have never chosen to have cancer. Now that I am on this side, I can say I would not choose to have missed what God showed me along the way.

Isaiah 43:1 says, "Fear not, for I have redeemed you; I have summoned you by name; you are mine." This verse soon became my favorite, and it was what I went to in times of need. The fact that He calls me by my name is incredible. I do not feel worthy.

CHAPTER 10
I Saw God in a Pink Jersey

After my initial ten-day stay in Houston, I was beat. I was tired. I just wanted to go home and be with my family. My two oldest, Hailey and Marcus, were home from school in Arkansas. There is nothing better when you are down than spending time with your family, and that's where I wanted to be: snuggled on the couch with my kiddos.

My youngest, Daniel, was still in junior high and he played select baseball. Let me tell you, if you have not experienced a travel team, it's a lot. The relationships you form, however, are amazing. Those teammates and their families were family to me. Daniel happened to have a tournament in San Marcos that weekend. In my thoughts, I wanted to just go home and have Daniel stay in Midland and not go to the tournament. God had a different plan. I must remember that His plan is always the best. Reluctantly, I decided to go ahead and go to the tournament, but I promise, I was kicking and screaming. I did not want to go.

We walked into the hotel lobby in San Marcos and the entire team was dressed in pink jerseys that said, "Playing for Paula." It was very emotional for me to see the love and support of that team. Then I looked in the back and saw Hailey and Marcus standing there. A friend who owned a plane picked them up and took them to the tournament so they could be there with me.

God also blessed my weekend with my brother and my sister-in law, Brad and Jill. They just so happened to be in San Marcos for the weekend and were able to watch some of Daniel's baseball games. Then God decided to bless me with even more family. My mother-in-law and father-in-law decided to come up for the weekend as well to see everyone. I told God I wanted to be with my family. He answered my prayer, but in a much bigger and better way than I could have ever imagined! Thank you, God, for surrounding me with family when I needed it the most.

We need to remember to thank God for His signs of love. God knows what we need before we do. He has you in the palm of His hand, and He will guide you down your confusing, twisted road. Even in the biggest storms of life, God has promised His love and faithfulness!

I love to think back often of the song "Goodness of God" to bring me back to perspective.

And all my life You have been faithful
And all my life You have been so, so good
With every breath that I am able
Oh, I will sing of the goodness of God.

CHAPTER 11
I Saw God in His Arms

My initial trip to MD Anderson was long and hard. It was a week and a half of mammograms, biopsies, scans, and much more. I can remember vividly to this day the last biopsy I had to undergo. It was an MRI guided biopsy, so the fear of an MRI and a biopsy combined was more than I could stand. I was waiting in a little room with a curtain drawn. I was crying out of fear and being tired of all the tests. When the nurse came in to get me, she saw my despair and quickly brought my husband in to comfort me.

The time came for my test. I remember lying on the table waiting to undergo the biopsy and feeling cold and alone. Realizing my overwhelming need for God to intervene, I started to pray for peace. I knew it had to be a peace that only God could provide.

At that moment, I literally felt God's arms around me. It was as if a warm blanket was covering me, like nothing else I had experienced. At one of my lowest times, God showed up. I remembered that every battle of mine is God's battle. I knew that God would go with me through this battle and fight right beside me. In this specific time, peace was given to me by my gracious Savior, and I started to cry uncontrollably. I remember my nurse asking if I was all right, and my response was, "Yes, I'm fine. These are happy tears." I knew she probably thought I had lost my marbles, but it didn't matter. I knew at that time He was waiting for me to just ask. He was waiting for me to fall into His arms. He was waiting to carry me through the next two years. At that moment, I knew He had chosen me, and I was His.

And the peace of God, which transcends all understanding, will guard
your hearts and your minds in Christ Jesus. (Philippians 4:7)

He who dwells in the shelter of the Most High will rest in the shadow of the Almighty. I will say
of the Lord, "He is my refuge and my fortress, my God, in whom I trust." (Psalm 91:1–2)

CHAPTER 12

I Saw God in a Nurse

The same nurse who had the compassion to go and get my husband when she noticed tears rolling down my cheeks is the same nurse who took the time to pray with me before my MRI. God, once again, put the exact person with me when He knew I would need her. He knows what we need before we do. I do not remember the exact words of that prayer, but now, looking back, God was putting me in the mindset to experience Him like I never had before.

I cannot thank this nurse enough for understanding my needs, fears, and anticipation. During my cancer, I was introduced to many people I never expected to meet, but I realized that God put them in my path. I often tell people that, at MD Anderson, it's like they make every employee take a "nice pill" each morning before the person shows up for work. Even if you look a little lost, there is someone asking if you need help.

In your time of trials and tribulation, remember to draw near to Him. James 4:8 says, "Come near to God and he will come near to you." *Nothing* can separate us from Him. We can never be in control of what God has in store for us; we do not know what tomorrow may bring. However, we can trust in His control.

When I am afraid, I will trust in you. In God, whose word I praise,
in God I trust; I will not be afraid. (Psalm 56:3–4)

CHAPTER 13
I Saw God in an Envelope

After returning from my initial visit to MD Anderson, the first thing on my to-do list was schedule the placement of my port to access my chemotherapy. This was to be done at our local hospital near my home. I remember being passed around from person to person trying to make the appointment. They kept telling us they would call us back with an appointment. When you know that cancer is in your body and you are fighting with all you have to survive, waiting until tomorrow for an appointment to be made is too long. My sweet husband once again fought for me. I remember that he went up to the office and told them he was not leaving until we had an appointment. Thanks to him, that appointment was made more quickly than expected.

The hospital called me and informed me that I needed to pay the remainder of what insurance would not pay before they could do my port procedure. Without really thinking, I moseyed on up to the hospital thinking, *Okay, I'll get this taken care of.* I do not remember the exact amount that we owed, but it was somewhere between $700 and $800. I did not know what to do. After a week and a half in Houston, we had paid for meals, hotels, gas, and a co-pay for every appointment. I knew at that time we would have to figure out how to make this payment. I told the receptionist that I would have to go home and talk to my husband and then get back with her.

Minutes later, we were sitting on the couch discussing our plan and figuring out how we would pay the bill. We heard the mail carrier deliver our mail. Alan got up and checked the mail. In the mailbox was a letter addressed to me with no return address on the envelope. I opened the envelope and there were ten $100 dollar bills inside. No note was attached. Someone wanted to remain anonymous and, in return, that person blessed us beyond what we could imagine. We both started to cry because, once again, God showed up. He answered a prayer that day—a prayer that we didn't even know a few hours before needed to be answered.

Sometimes, I know that it is a challenge to make the most of every minute of every day. However, serious news and details can make life take an immediate turn; it awakens us. We need to renew our hope in our never-failing, never-changing Father. Then, our strength will be refreshed, and our purpose will be redefined. You can do it; hang in there and remember that God honors those who are faithful to His calling. The Lord knows all you are going through. He loves you, He cares for you, and He will make sure not one detail is overlooked in your life. Psalm 56:8 reminds us that He collects every tear in a bottle, and Psalm 34:18 lets us know that He knows every hurt in our hearts.

But you are a chosen people, a royal priesthood, a holy nation, a people belonging to God, that you may declare the praises of him who called you out of darkness into his wonderful light. (1 Peter 2:9)

CHAPTER 14
I Saw God in My Chemo Buddies

Not long after I received my port, chemotherapy was underway. I was to have three months of a less aggressive chemo followed by a more aggressive chemo the next three months. I never had to go to one of my treatments alone. Every single time, someone was by my side. It was easily a four-hour visit each time. It started with drawing and checking my blood to make sure my counts were good enough to receive treatment. I am blessed to have stayed healthy throughout all my chemotherapy, never once having to reschedule a treatment due to my counts being too low. While they were checking my counts, I would put a numbing cream on my port to help with the pain of administering the port. The chemo was put right into my bloodstream through a catheter. Over a three-hour period, I would receive a saline solution for hydration as well as a steroid that would help with nausea and inflammation. Finally, I would receive my chemo.

Walking with cancer can be lonely. It was so nice to have someone who loved me sitting with me during those times. I am forever grateful for all who signed up to be my chemo buddies so I would not be alone. I know you had to sacrifice a big chunk of your day to sit with me. I will be forever blessed by our time together.

Sometimes, I wonder if Jesus ever felt alone. He traveled with his apostles, and he spoke to many crowds, but I wonder if they really understood the true intent of his mission. People would come to him often asking for earthly things, like healing and food. Dealing with earthly problems and being separated from his Heavenly Father had to have been hard. Then, I think of his last hours when no one stepped up to bat for him. All his closest friends denied him. He was abandoned. His disciples abandoned him while He was praying, as they were falling asleep. Even when He was on the cross, He had to have felt alone.

Psalm 21:6 reminds me, "Surely you have granted him eternal blessings and made him glad with the joy of your presence."

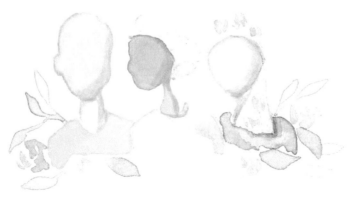

CHAPTER 15
I Saw God in a Bald Head

With each round of chemotherapy, I knew that losing my hair was right around the corner. The emotional impact, especially to a woman, of losing your hair is unimaginable. It is a symbol to the whole world that you have cancer. When strangers see you, will they do a double take? Will they try not to look at you at all? Will you hear the children asking their mothers, "Why does that lady have no hair?"

About two weeks after my first infusion, I started to see the hair on my pillow each morning. Seeing the hair in the shower, on the bathroom floor or in my brush was difficult. I got to the point where I was too scared to wash or even brush my hair for fear more and more would fall out. What was I holding on to? Why is our hair so important? We all know that it's part of our identities. It helps make us who we are.

I finally realized the inevitable, and it got to the point I couldn't handle the hair loss one more day. A sweet friend, Bonnie Eckles, and her daughter came over to help. We sat on the back porch, and she cut my hair. She knew the support and the encouragement I would need, and God could not have picked a better friend for me that day. She quickly dressed my head in a little hat because she knew the first look in the mirror would be unbearable.

About two weeks later, it was time to go down to the scalp. Once again, friends and a fantastic support group were there for me. Janet Smith, Teri Foulds, and my precious daughter took me to a salon that specializes in cutting hair for cancer patients. Seeing the final product was hard, but having it gone was a wonderful feeling. It was so much more comfortable, and the sight of clumps of hair were gone. I had to remember not to be afraid because I knew that God was in control.

Luke 12:7 says, "Indeed, the very hairs of your head are all numbered. Don't be afraid; you are worth more than many sparrows." Just to think that every hair that fell off my head and every clump that was on my pillow, God knew the exact amount. If He takes the time to know this small detail about me, I know His love for me is even greater than I can imagine.

CHAPTER 16
I Saw God in a Mirror

I've never had long hair. It has always been short. My mother grew up in an era when she had her hair fixed at the beauty shop once a week. Since my mom didn't really know how to fix my hair, long hair was never in the cards for me as a child. As a little girl, I would wrap a towel around my head just to pretend I had long hair. I would let the towel hang down and flutter back and forth, as if it was hair. Why is hair such a part of who we are? Why do we put so much emphasis on our hair? It doesn't matter if you are male or female. Your hair defines who you are. It also defines what era of time you are in. I love looking back at all the pictures of hair in the 80s. Wow! Did we have big hair, or what?

My sweet friend, Susan Rock, who gave me the elephant, knew the insecurities I would soon be facing with losing my hair. Another one of her many gifts was a mirror. She brought that mirror to school one day and told me that every time I looked in the mirror, I would know I was strong, beautiful, and loved. Looking in a mirror and telling yourself those things can be life changing. It doesn't matter if you are going through hard times or not. Having the strength to say those things to yourself will make you a different person. Because of Him, I felt strong. I felt beautiful. I felt loved. It just took someone special, like Susan, to help me see it.

I cannot convey the amount of love that was poured out on me. The support was overwhelming. Romans 12:15 says, "Rejoice with those who rejoice, mourn with those who mourn." God provided friends and loved ones to be with me in the times of rejoicing as well as the times of weeping.

Psalm 29:11 tells us, "The Lord gives strength to his people; the Lord blesses his people with peace."

CHAPTER 17
I Saw God on my Front Porch

Who doesn't like a gift, right? I can remember Christmas mornings when I was a child like it was yesterday. I remember my brothers and me getting in trouble year after year for waking up in the middle of the night to go downstairs and peek at what Santa brought. We often would be caught by Mom and Dad. They would make us stay in our rooms the next morning until we had permission to come out. Forgetting our punishment from the previous years before, we couldn't resist tiptoeing down the stairs the following year, just hoping not to be caught this time.

I feel as if our souls somehow, to some extent, remain like children. Even though I was forty-six at the time of my diagnosis, I knew inwardly I still had not grown up. My feelings are still hurt when I am not invited somewhere. I still like to snack on dessert before dinner. I still run to my mom when I am upset. In addition, I still like receiving gifts.

One special person knew the importance of a little something special when a friend is having a hard time. This sweet soul would leave me small gifts, Scripture, and little notes on my front porch. To this day, I still don't know who she was. The only reason I say it was a "she" is from the handwriting. I still have those notes of encouragement and little cards with Scripture. They were gifts from her to me that gave me more encouragement than one could imagine. It was a little something to get me through the day or week. It was like Christmas morning each day for my husband and me both. We loved the joy of peeking on the porch to see if she left me anything that day. Whoever you are, thank you for being so kind and taking the time to make me feel special and loved.

I just prayed that through my journey I could remember to trust like a child. Even though my body was tired, and I had no energy, I knew I had to trust God like I trusted my parents as a child. I knew He would not turn me away. I knew that in all my brokenness, I had to trust in Him.

Psalm 46:10–11 says, "Be still, and know that I am God; I will be exalted among the nations, I will be exalted in the earth. The Lord Almighty is with us."

Romans 8:26 says, "In the same way, the Spirit helps us in our weakness. We do not know what we ought to pray for, but the Spirit himself intercedes for us with groans that words cannot express."

CHAPTER 18
I Saw God in a Scarf

During my initial stay at MD Anderson, I learned I would have to endure chemotherapy. I had the decision of going the wig route or the scarf route. Immediately, I started people-watching in the hospital and noticing other women who were also going through chemo to see which route they chose. When I noticed others who were wearing scarves on their bald heads—nearly every woman who walked by—I had the thought that they looked absolutely beautiful. I decided then not to bother with a hot wig, as it was nearing the summer months. Being a woman means having the desire to look beautiful. The hunt for scarves became real. I think I collected nearly forty scarves. Some I bought; some were given to me as gifts. I had to have one for every outfit. Right? With that decision came trying to figure out how in the world they tied those scarves to make them look so beautiful.

That's when my sweet, precious daughter came to my rescue. I was so blessed to have her home the summer I was going through chemo. She would spend time Googling and looking at YouTube to find a different way to tie my scarf each day. All I would have to do was tell her it was time to "fix my hair," and she was on it. The time we spent together each morning, I will forever treasure. Thank you, God, for giving me a daughter who loves me like she does. I cherished that time with her before she had to go back to school in the fall.

During that summer, my husband and I were looking over her shoulder one day as she was sitting on the couch. She was on her computer trying to transfer to a college that was closer to home than her current college. It would be her senior year, and she was willing to forgo her last year at school with her friends to be closer to me. My husband and I had to have a very hard parenting moment. We told her she was going back to Arkansas, and she was not sacrificing her final year of school. Her sacrificial mind had the idea that she would be closer to home to help around the house when she could, but we did not want her to regret losing her senior year of college. Thank you, Hailey Jo, for having a sacrificial attitude and having the love and desire to help your mother.

Hard parenting moments are difficult, but the hard parenting moments when life throws you a curveball are even worse. Each morning when I got out of bed, I had the thought that I did not sign up for this. God signed me up for it instead. He gave me a daughter who did her very best to make me feel beautiful. He gave me a daughter who would help drain my tubes after surgery. He gave me a daughter who cared more about her mother than herself.

He called me to walk this road, and I wanted this experience to be life changing. I desired to be changed and to grow in Him. My desire was to figure out a way to honor Him through this time.

Jeremiah 17:14 reminds me, "Heal me, O LORD, and I will be healed; save me and I will be saved, for you are the one I praise."

CHAPTER 19
I Saw God in a Stranger's Kind Words

During my first round of chemo, I had a standing appointment every Wednesday at 1:00. This gave me time to teach a half-day and still have time to get home, change, and get out the door. Most of the other patients would have their infusions at the same time each week as well. Needless to say, it's easy to get to know others walking the same road you are. It's a blessing to see those relationships form. There's something to be said about two people walking a difficult path together. The bond is unexplainable.

Another blessing I had through this journey was my chemo buddies, friends who would graciously take me to my chemo appointments and sit with me. One particular week I remember quite well. I was with my chemo buddy, Melissa Matthews. I went back to have my blood checked. While I was gone, one of my fellow infusion friends asked Melissa why I was always in a good mood. She told Melissa that every time she saw me, I was one of the only ones with a positive attitude, and she could not comprehend why. She could not figure out how one going through cancer can be so happy.

You see, I knew every time I walked into a room, others would be assessing how I felt and how I chose to walk this journey. Indeed, I knew that I had to hold my head up high and walk this journey with the honor that God chose me to walk this road with Him. I had the desire for others to see God in me during this difficult time.

John 9 tells a story of a man who had been born blind. The disciples asked Jesus if it was the sins of the blind man or the sins of his parents that caused this unfortunate problem. Back in biblical times, it was common to believe that your sins caused an illness or an unfortunate circumstance. In verse 3, Jesus replied by saying, "'Neither this man nor his parents sinned' said Jesus, 'but this happened so that the work of God might be displayed in his life.'"

Guys, every road we walk is for God. It's always for His glory, whether we are on the mountaintop or in the valley. I knew I had to get to the point that I had to give Him the praise He deserved no matter what the circumstances were. I knew I had to thank Him each and every day for this road I was on. In return, God gave me unexplainable peace. The best way to receive this peace is to thank God while you are walking your difficult road. It took time for me to get to this place in my relationship with God. I was confused, hurt, and angry at first, but I soon realized that God created me, and as He knit me together in my mother's womb, He knew I would be walking this road. I realized that I had to view my cancer as a gift and that God chose *me* to walk this road with Him. For that, I am forever grateful.

In life, we will have problems of all sorts. Some will be very small. Some will be large. We need to practice when we are having a small problem not to focus on our circumstances, but on God. If we do this continually, when bad situations arise, it will be second nature to turn to God. When problems arise, we need to surrender them to God. This will put space between our circumstances and ourselves, and we can focus on Him more clearly. We will face trials in our lives. James 1:2 tells us to "consider it pure joy, my brothers, whenever you face trials of many kinds." Notice he didn't say if, but when.

"I have told you these things, so that in me you may have peace. In this world you will have trouble. But take heart! I have overcome the world." (John 16:33)

CHAPTER 20
I Saw God in a Quilt

When going through chemo, I quickly found out the importance of being surrounded with comforting things. I would always pack a bag with things to make me feel more at home, such as hard candy and lip balm to help with dry mouth from chemo. My journal and a good book were always packed. Of course, I would bring snacks. Everyone loves a good snack to get his or her mind off things. The most treasured thing I brought from home was a prayer quilt that my mother-in-law so carefully made for me. I love that quilt for two reasons. First, the fact that she loved me enough to put the time and effort into that work of art warmed my heart and strengthened me. Second, the purpose of the quilt was to have my loved ones write a prayer or an encouraging message on it. All during my treatments, and even at home, I was physically surrounded by sweet words from the people God put in my life to walk this journey with me.

I am so blessed to have had Connie with me during my journey. From her sweet gifts and selfless acts of kindness, God knew I needed her to walk with me. One of the biggest reasons it was nice to have her beside me was her medical knowledge. She was able to go into the doctor's office with me and ask questions that we did not know needed to be asked. My mind would be stuck on one word or phrase from the doctor, but she was able to keep listening and comprehending what they would say. Connie, because of you, I am forever grateful.

I am not sure I will ever take up the art of quilting. There is so much intricate work and creativity that goes into the quilt, and I guess I don't have the patience to stick with a project for that long. Cutting all those small pieces only to sew them back together is overwhelming and a true act of love.

God is the master when it comes to sewing. Remember, He knit us together in our mother's wombs. How comforting is it to know that He's the Master Creator? I know that He has a unique plan for me and you. He will take all those tiny pieces of your messed-up life and sew them back together. What a wonderful gift. What is miraculous is that He doesn't even need a pattern. He knows exactly how and when to sew each piece together and the quilt will be absolutely beautiful and perfect each and every time. What is even more amazing is that each quilt that he puts together is unique in its own way. Every stitch He adds is perfect and every stitch he stitches is at just the right time.

There was a particular verse that played a huge part in my journey. Psalm 139:5 says, "You hem me in-behind and before; you have laid your hand upon me." It is comforting to know that while God is stitching us back together, he takes the time to hem us in. He is behind us and before us during our journeys. If you search, you will be able to feel his hand upon you.

Psalm 139:13–16 says,

For you created my inmost being; you knit me together in my mother's womb. I praise you because I am fearfully and wonderfully made; your works are wonderful, I know that full well. My frame was not hidden from you when I was made in the secret place. When I was woven together in the depths of the earth, your eyes saw my unformed body. All the days ordained for me were written in your book before one of them came to be."

God knew before you were born the difficult journeys you would walk in your lifetime. However, know that He has spent your lifetime preparing you for those journeys.

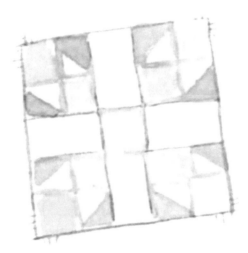

CHAPTER 21
I Saw God in a Song

My first round of less intense chemotherapy drugs was once a week for three months. When it was time to start my next round, I would receive an infusion once every three weeks. It was brutal and took all three weeks to feel better, just to start it all over again. The name of the medication was Adriamycin, commonly known as the Red Devil. It was bright red in color, but I can honestly say it acted like the Devil. One will experience nausea, sores in the mouth and down the throat, damage to nails and skin, damage to the heart, severe lethargy, loss of taste, and many more symptoms. I literally did not have the strength on the evening of my infusion to turn my head from one side of the pillow to the next. Adriamycin had to be administered manually by my infusion nurse rather than from the bag hanging from the IV pole as it had been administered in the past. The reason was that if one drop of the Adriamycin dropped on my skin, my skin would melt. Now remember, these medications are going directly into our bloodstreams, but in order to survive we choose to go through with it.

I will forever be grateful for my church that held me up during my journey. The week before I started the Red Devil, the elders of the church and loved ones gathered around to pray and lift me up to give me much needed strength. The support I had through my journey is unexplainable.

A song that got me through some of my hardest days is called "Praise you in This Storm" by Casting Crowns. The lyrics of the song remind us that in each storm we are in, God will never leave our sides. He will grab hold of every tear that we cry and hold each one near to His heart. We need to remember that when God does this for us, we need to praise Him, even when it doesn't seem possible.

I remember vividly the first day of my Red Devil treatment. Fear was in every thought. Every person reacts differently to each treatment, and the unknown of how I would react frightened me. My chemo buddy that day was a friend named Alyssa. When she came to the door to get me, I was trembling out of fear. As I got into the car, I heard a familiar song on the radio: "Praise you in This Storm." Once again, God showed up with another wink so I would know everything was going to be all right.

Remember to praise God in your storms. He will hold every tear and will never leave your side. Nothing, and I mean nothing, can separate us from the love of God. Keep this thought at the front of your mind each time you experience fear or anxiety. Do not think you are not loved, but remember how incredibly you are loved. He will never leave us or forsake us.

Joshua 1:5–6 reminds us, "I will be with you; I will never forsake you. Be strong and courageous."

I Saw God in a Little Clothing Store

In my many trips back and forth to Houston, I would often fly down there in the morning and fly back in the evening all for one thirty-minute appointment. It was always encompassed by delicious food at a good restaurant and a little shopping at the fun stores. The airport was close to the hospital, so it was easy to get back and forth. I remember one particular trip I made was on a Thursday. My friend Bonnie flew to Houston with me. By the way, that was another way God blessed me. I never had to make that trip alone. There were always the finances, donated by many unknown friends, to help with trips and stays. Bonnie and I got off the plane and went to pick up our car. Would you know, it was a little red Mustang. We thought we were so cool! It was a fun day running around Houston in that little car.

What seemed like a normal routine visit turned into somewhat of a nightmare. After my mastectomy, several weeks prior, my incision was having a hard time healing. During the visit on that Thursday, my surgeon ended up opening the incision up in the office to try to clean it out and proceeded to restitch it—all in his office! It turned out to be quite comical. The doctor needed light and the only extra light we had was the flashlight on Bonnie's phone. Poor thing: she was standing there trying to give the doctor the much-needed light as he was barking orders to the nurse. I am glad God chose to add a little comic relief to a somewhat stressful situation. Because of him opening me up in the office, I was then stuck in the hospital for forty-eight hours of IV antibiotics. That was not in our game plan. Bonnie helped get me checked in to the hospital, but then she had no choice but to head back to Midland to get back to her family and work, leaving me by myself.

Leave it to my sweet husband to figure out what to do next. He got on the phone and found a Midland friend who "just so happened" to be in Houston. She stopped by my room and got my clothes and washed them for me. I was not planning on being there overnight, so I had nothing with me. He called other friends, Kim and Susan, who lived nearby to visit with me during my stay. He was a little worried about me being by myself. I figured I could go home after my forty-eight hours, but my doctor wanted to see me the following Monday. I tried to inform him that I had no clothes, no personal items, and no make-up—nothing. He wasn't too concerned with my make-up or my apparel and told me I had to stay. My cousin Karen came to the rescue. Karen lived about an hour and a half from Houston. She picked me up, took me to Target, and set me up with the personal items I needed. Then we went back to her house for the weekend. I decided to just borrow clothes from her and not have the expense of buying them. What girl turns down a very good excuse to buy new clothes?

We decided on Saturday to make a trip into Bryan, Texas and do a little running around and go to lunch. I remembered I had a good friend, Elisa, who owned a clothing store in Bryan, so we decided to stop by for a quick visit. You would have thought I was the Queen of England. My friend treated me like royalty and fixed me up with outfits to help me through my stay. Once again, God showed up in that little clothing store with my friend.

That isolated incident made me aware of the relationships that God put in my life for a purpose. I am forever grateful for my friends who walked beside, me even in the many not-so-fun times. Ephesians 3:20 reminds us, "Now to him who is able to do immeasurably more than all we ask or imagine, according to his power that is at work within us." I would have been just fine borrowing my cousin's clothes for the weekend, but God went above and beyond to make me feel good about myself. He graciously gave me more support from the people He placed in my life. Once again, He thought about the small details. Even the little things that we think are unimportant are important to Him.

CHAPTER 23

I Saw God in a Cousin

About five years prior to my diagnosis, my cousin Sharon underwent breast cancer treatment as well. We were both forty-six when we were diagnosed. We had previously experienced the death of her sister Lee Ann and the death of our sweet Aunt Jo to breast cancer. Our sweet Aunt Wanda had beaten breast cancer, praise be to our God. Sharon and I were both tested for the BRCA gene. We were surprised to find out that neither of us had the gene because breast cancer was so prevalent on our side of the family.

Knowing that Sharon had walked the same journey just a few years before me, it was nice to be able to call her when I had questions or concerns, or in times of need. I feel so blessed to have had her shoulder to cry on. Sharon was so thoughtful in her words and gifts. She sent me a little James Avery bracelet as a constant reminder that God was in control, and He was in charge of this journey.

In one of my journal entries I wrote, "Best day yet. After talking to Cousin Sharon last night so many concerns and questions were answered. I had a wonderful day! Yesterday, not such a good day, but look at all the many blessings God poured my way to comfort me. My God is good."

Whatever path God has chosen for you, whatever journey you are about to face, remember that it is God's path, God's journey. When we have the knowledge to realize this, and when we have the understanding that it is not our journey, but His, He will carry us to places we cannot fathom. I realize that letting go of the reins is difficult, but remember that he commands us to "trust in the LORD with all your heart and lean not on your own understanding; in all your ways acknowledge him, and he will make your paths straight" (Proverbs 3:5–6).

CHAPTER 24
I Saw God in Yummy Meals

Between six months of chemo and six surgeries, we were fed for nearly two years by people who unselfishly brought meals over weekly. And guys, I'm talking about the good meals. It was two years of yummy comfort food. My loved ones know how to cook. We absolutely did not go hungry. I actually think my husband and I put on twenty pounds in those two years—but it was so worth it! I remember homemade rolls, a delicious roast, smoothies, yummy desserts, and much more. We even had a beef tenderloin shipped from Perini Ranch in Abilene. If you have not had one of their beef tenderloins, you have not lived. It is beyond good. Each meal was made with the loving hands of my friends. Their generosity, love, and concern was greatly appreciated.

If you are not living in community, you need to be. I am not sure what my road would have looked like if I had not been in community. You cannot wait until you're thrown a fast ball. You must be prepared by being involved and having a foundational relationship with your God and Savior. I had my God-given family, my school family, my church family, and friends who still today I consider family. I was blessed almost every day with my community through food, texts, cards, hugs, tears, visits, and phone calls. Let me tell you, it's hard to be the recipient of these gifts. It is a humbling experience. We all like being on the other side of giving. There is no way to thank them properly for carrying you through the journey. Be open to receiving their gifts with open arms.

I would look at these gifts and remember the greatest gift of all. Christ gave us the gift of eternal life. This is a gift that cannot be purchased or bought. It is free to all who accept it. The cost has already been paid. The death of our Christ on the cross paid for our eternal lives. I think about that every day and cannot comprehend how or why I was given this gift. It is hard to be a recipient of a gift like this because I know I do not deserve it. However, with grace, this gift is mine, and it can be yours too.

For the wages of sin is death, but the gift of God is eternal life in Christ Jesus or Lord. (Romans 6:23)

CHAPTER 25
I Saw God in a Party

I am not a runner, by any means. I don't think anyone in my entire family is. To have the privilege of running a literal race and crossing the finish line is a rush that I cannot relate to. Now, crossing a finish line after a fight against cancer is a rush I can relate to. Each finish line, each accomplishment, was just as sweet as the one before. The treatments were followed with a huge check mark. It was such a good feeling to cross off my infusions on the calendar, followed by crossing off radiation treatments.

The last chemotherapy treatment I received was October 31. You always hear of a chemo patient ringing his or her bell, but to experience it is so sweet. I had never rung a bell before with such anticipation and excitement. I am sure I rang it way too long and way too hard, and the others listening to the bell ring were glad when I stopped. I didn't care; I was proud of my accomplishment. My sweet husband and my mother had beautiful flowers awaiting my last chemo. I still remember my sweet friends Lori Thomas and Angie Rohwer were with me for that special ring.

Friends of mine decided to throw me a "No Mo' Chemo" party to celebrate this huge finish line. They fixed all my favorites, and everyone showed up in pink. What a celebration we had! No more chemo is something to celebrate. I would not have survived without this group of friends, and as usual, they knew just what I needed. The food, the fellowship, and the laughter was just what the doctor ordered.

Paul says in 2 Timothy 4:7, "I have fought the good fight, I have finished the race, I have kept the good faith." Paul was in prison in Rome when he wrote this book and was nearing his last days. He was writing this second letter to his dear friend Timothy. I think Paul felt as if he would not get out of prison, and these were his last words he wanted to convey to the ones he loved. He reminds us in verse 8 that "there is in store for me the crown of righteousness, which the Lord, the righteous Judge, will award to me on that day-not only to me, but also to all who have longed for his appearing." When you fight your fight and when you finish your race, you will also have the crown of righteousness that He has promised. Finish strong, wherever you are in your battle, and know that He is fighting right beside you.

CHAPTER 26
I Saw God in My Mother

The next thing on my agenda after chemo was my mastectomy. It was scheduled for December 6. I had a month to recover from my last dose of Adriamycin. The date of my surgery ended up being good timing, and as I have learned, God's timing is always perfect. We had just been to my mother's house in East Texas for Thanksgiving. It was so good seeing my extended family for a lengthy stay. We headed straight from East Texas to Houston for surgery and just so happened to be able to find friends who were also celebrating the holiday nearby who could take Daniel, my son, back to Midland for us.

Even though traveling was hard physically and emotionally for my mom, she would drive all the way to Midland to help in whatever way she could after each of my surgeries. I cherished this sweet time with my mother. We all love being spoiled by our loved ones. In my journal entry on the way home from surgery, I wrote:

> No matter how old you get, a mother's love never diminishes. I know she most likely is worried about me but seeing how much she cares gives me so much comfort. I cannot wait to see my mommy and hug her neck. Why do we always want our mothers when we are sick or hurt? Thank you, God, for mothers as caring and as nurturing as my mommy.

> God blessed my mom with the gift of hospitality. Having her nearby after a surgery was the best. That lady can cook! It was so nice to have her nearby to be able to experience her wonderful cooking. She blessed us even further by doing laundry and light housekeeping. I know it was hard for her to witness me in this state. I could not even imagine. Nevertheless, she was a rock. Galatians 6:2 tells us to "carry each other's burdens, and in this way, you will fulfill the law of Christ." Thank you, God, for giving me my mother to help carry the burden. I love you.

> Being a family means you are a part of something very wonderful. It means you will love and be loved for the rest of your life. (Lisa Weed)

CHAPTER 27
I Saw God in Roommates

In February, I headed to Houston to live for seven weeks. I am very grateful to have been able to have my chemo at Texas Oncology in Midland. However, my oncologist thought it would be in my best interest to have my radiation at MD Anderson. My doctor reminded me that a team of radiation oncologists would together design my treatment plan. I packed up my car and headed to Houston. It was extremely hard being separated from my husband and my youngest child, but we made the best of it, trying to see each other every other weekend.

I was blessed to be able to live in a furnished apartment for the time I was in Houston. A local church in Houston had bought several apartments close to the hospital and rented them out for a minimal price. It was small; let's just say it was very cozy. But it did the job, and I was very grateful that my commute to the hospital was short. The apartment came with a completely furnished kitchen, and it was a one bedroom with two twin beds. Perfect for a roommate to stay and keep me company. Over the course of the seven weeks, there may have been only one night that I had to stay by myself. I was blessed to have family and friends come in and out to stay with me and keep me company. Before long, I was their local travel agent. I quickly learned all the fun places to eat and the best places to shop. The local rodeo was going on while I was there, and that was a favorite activity to do with guests. I literally could walk across the street and go to the stock show and rodeo, which was followed by a concert with many great artists.

One of my journal entries from my stay in Houston read,

God-you are so gracious to me, beyond explanation. I am a being destined to fall- but you are right there extending your mercy, time and time again. You are my rock, my steady, and my hope. I find comfort and peace in knowing that you come to me with everything I need before I know I need it. You are beyond capable of healing. I will call upon your name whenever I feel weak and weary. Thank you, Heavenly Father, for each and every person you put in my path during my stay in Houston. Each friend or family member met a specific need. In Jesus name, Amen.

God's love will be evident through your friends and family during your journey. These relationships can enrich your life in ways you cannot comprehend. They can encourage you when you need it, and they will be there to celebrate with you when you cross those finish lines. You will see throughout your journey that God will place different people at different points to accomplish different needs. He knows who and what you need before you do. Let God be seen through them.

Remember as you are in the midst of your hardships to search for Him. Take time to be still and look for the ways He has blessed you and the many blessings to follow. You will find that He can be seen in places you never expected.

Be joyful always; pray continually; give thanks in all circumstances, for this is God's will for you in Christ Jesus. (1 Thessalonians 5:16–18)

CHAPTER 28

I Saw God in Someone Paying it Forward

Living my whole married life in Midland, Texas has been great. While it may not be the prettiest town in the world—okay, it's downright ugly—it is a great place to raise a family. When people come to visit for the first time, my husband and I tell them to drive in at night; hoping they won't see just how ugly it really is. We always justify it by saying the sunsets are beautiful. They really are. For a midsize town, Midland has pretty good restaurants. However, living in Houston for seven weeks made me realize there are so many restaurants I don't get to experience as often as I'd like, and some restaurants I didn't even know existed.

One of the weeks during my stay, my mom came down to be with me. I am very grateful for my cousin Karen. She lived close enough to Houston to come down and help or just to spend the day. After radiation one day, we three decided to go shopping and eat dinner. We chose the restaurant Pei Wei that evening. We were just about finished with our meal, and I asked for the check. We were informed that a stranger paid for our meal. I wanted to thank the person, but my server said the person was already gone. What a blessing they were to me that day!

God chose that day to put a stranger in our path to bless us. He knows just what we need at just the right time. I didn't know that day how special that moment would be to me. God is all around you. You just need to remember to stop long enough to see him. He presented Himself in a stranger that day.

One day He presented Himself in a lady checking us out in the cafeteria at MD Anderson. She must have noticed my demeanor and asked if she could pray with me. Here we were, going through the busy line in the cafeteria, and she paused and said a prayer with me. Wow! Another unforgettable blessing!

I do not remember my extenuating circumstances from those experiences, but I do know that nothing is too difficult for us. God will choose others to accomplish His purpose, and it is up to us to realize the little "God winks" and know He is behind us, before us, and beside us. When we are down and troubled and we feel weak, our weaknesses are designed to open us up to His power. Whatever road you are walking, I challenge you to be still. Be still in the Lord and wait on Him. He will show up.

Romans 8:38–39 says,

For I am convinced that neither death nor life, neither angels nor demons, neither the present nor the future, nor any powers, neither height nor depth, nor anything else in all creation, will be able to separate us from the love of God that is in Christ Jesus our Lord.

CHAPTER 29

I Saw God in 350 Square Feet

The end of radiation was near, and I was on my last week of treatment. It could not have come any sooner. Between the three exit wounds from radiation on my back and the burns on my front side, I could hardly get dressed. I honestly did not know if I could do another treatment. God had a great game plan to distract me. It was spring break, so it was perfect timing for my husband and children to join me in Houston. My two oldest, Hailey and Marcus, drove in from school in Arkansas, and Alan and Daniel flew in from Midland. It was a tight squeeze, but we made it work and loved being all cooped up together.

During that week, I received a phone call from my brother Brad. He said he and his family were coming down from Dallas for a couple of days to join us. Okay, we were already crammed in that little apartment, but now we were really crammed. Each night it was like a sea of bodies in that living room. There was no getting up in the middle of the night to use the restroom because we were too afraid of stepping on someone. However, what fun we had! We did the whole stock show/rodeo/concert thing and had more fun than you can imagine. I enjoyed the laughter and the conversation. Thank you, God, for knowing what I needed and placing much needed time with family in my week.

Friday, March 13, 2015 was the day to ring the bell once again. I will never forget that ring. I was *all finished* with treatment. All my treatments were complete! No more chemo! No more radiation! The freedom, joy, and excitement I experienced was exhilarating. I am forever grateful that all nine of us were there together to ring that bell. What a sacrifice it was for Brad and his family to give up their spring break just to come ring a bell with me. Being with me as I crossed this amazing finish line was more important than any spring break, and I am glad to have experienced that day with them.

Brad and I live over five hours apart, so seeing each other is hard. Throughout this difficult journey, however, he always knew when to pop in and help. I remember him sleeping all night in a chair in a hospital room to give Alan a break. He and his sweet wife Jill sat with me in the hospital during a blood transfusion. I remember after a surgery, he made me walk one more time around the nursing station so my strength could improve. Thank you, Lord, for my brother and his family's sacrificial love.

Proverbs 17:17 says, "A friend loves at all times, and a brother is born for a time of adversity." Here Solomon is talking about the value of a true friend and a brother. Each will be there to love you in the good times and the trying times.

CHAPTER 30
I Saw God in a Tattoo

My middle child, Marcus, must be the best gift giver ever. Each Christmas and birthday, the thought he puts into each gift is incredible. It was Christmas 2014 and I had just completed chemo about seven weeks prior. Marcus had the idea to buy a cap and he had my initials monogrammed on it. What guy thinks to do that? He also knows the brand of serving dishes I love, and he will search high and low to find just the right one for his mother. During Christmas at the Gower house, we open gifts one at a time. We start from the youngest and go to the oldest. It takes a while, but what joy it brings us to be able to see the expression when our loved ones open gifts from us. Marcus, I know, takes joy from that.

One gift that Marcus gave me I will never forget. He was home for the weekend, and we were sitting on the couch catching up. He pulled up his shirt, and I saw a tattoo on his chest. The Roman numerals read III XIII MMXV. Now mind you, I am horrible at reading Roman numerals. As you can imagine, I was trying to figure out the meaning behind these numerals. I got the three and the thirteen, but there was no way I was going to understand the 2015. I do know I totally ruined the moment because he had to explain to me the meaning of the tattoo. It's kind of like having to explain a joke. It totally ruins the joke. The tattoo Marcus had on this chest was the date of my last treatment. What a gift. Of course, I cried—I cried like a baby. Thinking that he would do this for me and knowing that I have a child that cares for me like Marcus does helped me through my journey. Over the last few years, it has been a joy to see him mature into a man who loves the Lord and strives to show others that relationship by his actions.

There is a song by Matt Redman called "Never Alone" that touched me during my journey. The chorus says,
Never once did we ever walk alone
Never once did You leave us on our own
You are faithful, God, You are faithful.

This song brings Lamentations 3:22–23 to mind. It says, "Because of the Lord's great love we are not consumed, for his compassions never fail. They are new every morning; great is your faithfulness." I am grateful I had God to walk with during my journey, but I am also glad I had Marcus walking beside me.

CHAPTER 31

I Saw God in a Sacrificial Friend

When radiation was complete, it was time for my reconstruction surgery. After my mastectomy, a tissue expander was put in to hold the place until we could have the reconstructive surgery. My body rejected the tissue expander, and it had to come out before I could start radiation. Consequently, we were left with very few options and decided on the DIEP flap reconstruction. In this type of reconstruction, the surgeon uses tissue from the woman's belly to create a new breast. Basically, you get a tummy tuck in the process. There must be pros, right? The surgeon will relocate your fat tissue from your stomach to your breast and tie all the new blood vessels from your stomach tissue to the current ones in your chest. It is a very long process, but it is usually followed with great results.

What we were not expecting was, three days later, one of my blood vessels rejected the attachment of the other blood vessel. My tissue in my reconstructed breast was not receiving enough blood flow. Because of this, I was wheeled into an emergency surgery to try to repair the blood vessel. The surgeon was unsuccessful and had to remove the entire reconstructed breast, leaving me with just a thin skin graft covering the area.

My husband and mother-in-law had already been with me in Houston for over a week, which meant my youngest son was in Midland without his parents for an extended time, staying with friends. After some discussion, Alan and my mother-in-law decided to go back home to be with Daniel. A precious friend, Sharla Free, came to Houston to stay with me to relieve Alan and basically take the baton. Sharla stayed with me in Houston for another week and a half or so. Her selfless care blessed me. She had to bathe me, push me around in a wheelchair, fix my hair (now grown back), and help me dress. She took care of every need I had.

After that surgery, my body rejected the skin graft. I was left with an open wound about four inches by six inches. This, unfortunately, ended in an infection so deep you could see my ribs. Sweet Sharla came over every morning for about six weeks at 5:00 a.m. to help me dress my wound. Now if you know Sharla, mornings are very slow for her. I get it. It takes time to wake up. For her to be at my house that early was a huge sacrifice.

I was at my lowest of lows at this time. I was so tired of being sick. I was tired of being tired. I was tired of being separated from my loved ones. I was tired of going to appointments. I was tired of talking to doctors.

I was tired of having cancer.

It's when you are at your lowest that God steps in even more. He put a friend in my life to pick me up when I was down, a friend to make me look my best when I could not. He put a friend in my life who loved me unconditionally. I needed the support of Sharla during that time. God put her in my life because He knew exactly what and who I needed. God showed up in a friend. I pray that God puts a Sharla in your life.

A man of many companions may come to ruin, but there is a friend
who sticks closer than a brother. (Proverbs 18:24)

"My command is this: Love each other as I have loved you. Greater love has no
one than this, that he lay down his life for his friends." (John 15:12)

CHAPTER 32

I Saw God in a Tear

The gift of family is a tremendous gift. All my life, my family has been intentional, sharing every other Thanksgiving with members of my extended family. I love being able to not only see my brothers and their families, but also be able to stay connected with cousins. We always have a good time at Thanksgiving. As you can imagine, an enormous spread of delicious food always graces the table. We visit, we eat, we go on walks, and we watch plenty of football. We especially like to play games. I cannot think of a get-together that a game of Risk was not the centerpiece of the dining room table. We may only get together every other year, but it is a blessed time.

One year, my brother Shawn couldn't be with us, so he sent a gift. You're thinking, how sweet, right? This gift was different. My middle brother Brad received a call from his office saying there was a package for him. He told his secretary that he would get it on Monday when he returned to work, to which she replied that his package may not be alive by Monday. Brad headed up to his office only to find that Shawn sent a live turkey for Thanksgiving in the mail. Who does that? My family knows how to have fun, but they also know how to be serious.

The Thanksgiving about two and a half years after my diagnosis, we were all in Dallas spending time once again at my brother Brad's house. While we were sitting enjoying our meal, Brad had each of us tell what or whom we were grateful for. My oldest brother Shawn reflected that he was thankful for my health and my victory over cancer. I will never be more appreciative of the tears falling down his cheek and the love expressed during that moment. Shawn lives in Portland, Oregon, a long, long way away from us. He had to be intentional with ways to help during my fight. He was so thoughtful during my journey to give me a little phone call at just the right time to let me know he was thinking of me. Alan and I would be on our way for an appointment in Houston, and Shawn would call with our hotel reservations. He would think of a need and take care of that need before we could. He was so helpful. I know he was a long way away, but he made the best of it. His love and support was perfect—just what we needed.

Sometimes, we must be intentional about the ways we help others. We may not know what to do or how to help, but every small act of service goes a long way. When helping someone with a need that seems overwhelming, you may not feel like you are helping the person very much on your end, but trust me, it doesn't go unnoticed. Think of a way you can bless someone today. It may just be a text or a phone call. Whoever God puts on your heart, follow through with that calling. Your blessing is a need. Follow your gut and follow your heart.

If you follow your heart and stay true to yourself, beautiful things will happen. (Shannon Kaiser)

"Peace I leave with you; my peace I give you. I do not give to you as the world gives.
Do not let your hearts be troubled and do not be afraid." (John 14:27)

CHAPTER 33

I Saw God in New York City

The end of my journey ended with a bang. After two years of treatment, surgeries, and recovery, I had eight precious friends take me to New York City to celebrate. It was a celebration worth having. I was so glad to be on this side of cancer. God had walked me through very difficult times, and now it was time to give Him thanks and time to celebrate. Lori Riggs, Marca Young, Deann McGraw, Sherry Peets, Sharla Simmons, Kelli Bateman, Sharla Free, Connie McGraw, and I all hopped on an airplane and off we went. We ate the best foods and saw the best shows. As many tourists do, we were lost a couple of times, then were lost again, but it was all worth it. It was the beginning of December, so New York City was decked out in all its best Christmas décor. We enjoyed just walking up and down the streets and looking in the windows. I can still remember how beautiful it all was. We would leave the hotel first thing in the morning and would return in the evenings beat from all the walking. Those tired feet were worth it! We had so much fun. I have so many sweet memories with eight friends who took time to celebrate and give their God credit for a journey that was worth fighting for. Thank you, God, for putting those ladies in my life.

The end of my journey was complete, and the time together and the laughter we experienced was healing. Proverbs 17:22 says, "A cheerful heart is good medicine."

A journal entry around this time said,

You are my God, and I will give you thanks; you are my God, and I will exalt you. Give thanks to the Lord, for he is good; his love endures forever. (Psalm 118:28–29)

Dear God, may I wake up fresh and renewed, ready to face the day. May I find the time to pause in Your presence, and listen for your voice, and give you thanks for all you've done and for all you're about to do. I am your beloved. I am yours. Your banner over me is love. Thank you, God, for giving me time to pause and remember who you are.

CHAPTER 34
I Saw God in a New Friend

In conclusion, I want to tell you a story about a new friend I recently had the pleasure of meeting. Her name is Lisa. In just the short time I have known her, she has blessed me beyond belief. I am convinced God puts different people in our paths at different times for a reason. God chose this specific time to put Lisa into my life.

We were sitting on the couch at my daughter's baby shower getting to know each other. Lisa's husband works with my daughter. I had heard nothing but good things about this sweet family, and I was excited to finally put faces to names. As many of you know, I cannot help but talk about the ways God blessed me through my journey and my newly formed ministry, One Bite at a Time. As we were discussing my ministry, Lisa told me a little bit about her journey.

Lisa had recently lost a sister-in-law to cancer. A loved one told her, "Just enjoy the journey. Don't worry about the end result." *Wow*! What a concept! No matter what journey you are in the middle of, or what journey is around the corner, enjoy your time. Enjoy this time with your precious Savior. Enjoy being in His arms and surrounded with His care. So many times, we try to rush and look to the end of our journeys to see what our lives will look like. This is just like my friend, Janet, asked me at the beginning of my journey how to eat an elephant. Her answer was one bite at a time. All you must do is focus on the now, your current bite. Do not look down to the end of the road and try to anticipate what your circumstances will be. Take time to stop and enjoy the journey. Stop long enough to see what God has done for you and see his blessings.

I related this story that Lisa shared with me to my daughter. My daughter asked me, "Mom! How do you enjoy the journey of cancer?" That is a very valid question. I proceeded to tell her with tears in my eyes that until you have walked a journey worth fighting for, you may not be able to see how that is possible. I told her that I would have never chosen to have cancer, but I am so glad that I walked that road because of what God showed me during that time. I have a completely different relationship with God, a relationship that I will cherish for the rest of my life. My journey made me who I am today. When a rough journey shows up unexpectedly, choose God and let Him show up. Remember, the journey is His.

Dedication

This book is dedicated to my family. Alan, Hailey, Marcus, and Daniel, thank you for being there with me during this walk. Without you guys and God, I wouldn't have made it. Love to you all. Thank you for being my rocks.

Printed in the United States
by Baker & Taylor Publisher Services